Copyright

Ninja Blender Recipe Bible: 50+ Delicious Recipes for your High Powered Blender

Disclaimer

The information provided in this book is designed to provide helpful information on the subjects discussed. This book is not meant to be used, nor should it be used, to diagnose or treat any medical condition. For diagnosis or treatment of any medical problem, consult your own physician. The publisher and author are not responsible for any specific health or allergy needs that may require medical supervision and are not liable for any damages or negative consequences from any treatment, action, application or preparation, to any person reading or following the information in this book. References are provided for informational purposes only and do not constitute endorsement of any websites or other sources. Readers should be aware that the websites listed in this book may change.

I recommend consulting a doctor to assess and/or identify any health related issues prior to making any dramatic changes to your diet and/or exercise regime.

Contents

Introduction

I want to thank you and congratulate you for downloading the book, *"Ninja Blender Recipe Bible."*

This book contains proven steps and strategies on how to make your own delectable smoothies, juices, pastries, soups, sauces, spreads, dressings, and desserts with your high-performance Ninja Professional Blender.

Ninja Professional Blender, as the name suggests, is ninja-fast and powerful! It's a high-performance, highly versatile blender with a sleek design. It's your perfect kitchen companion for juicing, pureeing, and crushing ice. Use this recipe Bible as your ultimate and perfect complement for your professional blender.

Thanks again for downloading this book, I hope you enjoy it!

Intro to Food Processing with the Ninja

Enjoy easy food processing, juicing, and pureeing with the Ninja Professional Blender. Featuring outstanding performance and sleek design, the Ninja perfectly crushes ice, whole fruits and vegetables in seconds. It incorporates Ninja Total Crushing Technology, powering it at a peak of 1000 watts. With its durable extra-large pitcher and powerful blades, it finds many uses beyond just pureeing. Use it for making smoothies, drinks, soups, and desserts for the whole family.

Benefits of Using the Ninja Professional Blender

High power

Power in wattage accounts for most of the performance of any blender. The Ninja Professional Blender has a built-in specially engineered motor that delivers power of up to 1000 watts. With such wattage, fruit blending and ice crushing can be done repeatedly with total ease. Whole vegetables are handled efficiently, thanks to its unparalleled motor strength. The motor speed is easy to adjust with just a press of any of the three buttons, plus one button for pulse spin.

Readily accessible recipes

With high versatility, it's easy to adapt your own favorite recipes you're used to with your previous blender. Moreover, you will save more time and enjoy food processing more. If it's your first home blender, then scan through a long list of recipes, not to mention everything we have here. There are so many recipes you can easily modify and experiment. The possibilities are endless.

Unique blade assembly

What adds to the Ninja's performance is its one-of-a-kind, state-of-the-art blade assembly. Unlike conventional blenders, the Ninja features a stem of blades that crushes ingredients evenly and thoroughly without the need for pushing ingredients down using a tamper. The ingredients are all processed, not only those on the bottom of the pitcher.

Dishwasher-safe parts

Many conventional blenders are sensitive to dishwasher and dishwashing liquid. Also, many people won't dare wash the blender manually because of its sharp blades that can easily lacerate hands. The Ninja gives you no worries. You can toss the blade assembly, the pitcher, and the lid into the dishwasher... and voila! You have your sparkly clean blender!

Free from Leaking

Are you afraid of possible leaks as with other blenders that typically have disjointed parts? Take the Ninja differently. There's no room for leaks and there will never be! The Ninja is only a single-piece appliance with just the blade assembly lightly mounted onto the base.

A very friendly price

At a decent price of around $100, it's a better choice over other exquisite gadgets. And it runs just as powerful as some more expensive, high-performance blenders.

Single set of blades

Some models on the market feature multiple blade sets for specific tasks (for crushing ice, grinding grains, for dry or wet ingredients, etc.), bringing about some complexity and hassle. Now, imagine an ultimate blender featuring just one set of blades—no need to change—that can do all the tasks. This is one of the many things that make the Ninja so convenient to use.

The Ninja strength

The Ninja is specially designed to withstand the test of time. Its durability allows you to have a lasting relationship with it, with less trouble and failure. Rest assured this awesome machine will continue to ease your food processing needs even with repeated and intense use. The Ninja is really a must-have for your kitchen.

Thrilling Smoothies and Juices

1. Prune Smoothie

1 cup apple juice or cider

1 1/2 cups finely cracked ice

1/2 cup soaked, pitted, dried prunes

Dash of cinnamon or Angostura

Insert the blade assembly in the Ninja pitcher and press Power button. Pour apple juice or cider into the Ninja pitcher. Add other ingredients. Place the lid properly and press the speed 2 button. Run machine for 2 minutes or until contents are thoroughly blended. Serve cold (yields 1 pint).

2. Grape-egg Smoothie

1/2 cup grape juice

1 tablespoon lime or lemon juice

1 teaspoon sugar or honey

1 egg

Always start with the blade assembly inserted in the Ninja pitcher. Pour grape juice and lemon juice into the Ninja pitcher. Secure the cover, turn on the machine, and press speed 2 button. Time machine for 2 minutes or until mixture is smooth. Pour contents into a glass and serve cold (yields 1 pint).

3. Milk Strawberry Smoothie

1 cup milk

1 pint fresh strawberries or 1 cup quick-frozen strawberries

4 tablespoons sugar

Pour milk into the Ninja pitcher. Add other ingredients. Add 1 cup of finely cracked ice for a chilled smoothie. Place the lid properly and press the power button. Press speed 2 and blend for 15 seconds to 2 minutes. Serve cold (yields about 1 pint). Note: For a richer drink, add one-half cup of ice cream or 2 marshmallows prior to blending.

4. Melon Smoothie

1 cup milk

1/2 cup diced honeydew

1 cup diced cantaloupe melon

Pour milk into the Ninja pitcher. Add honeydew and melon. Put the cover on the pitcher. Power up the machine and press the speed 2 button. Run machine for 15 seconds to 2 minutes. Serve cold in a glass (yields about 1 pint).

5. Carrot Milk Cocktail

1 cup milk

Dash salt

1/3 cup diced raw carrots

1 cup finely cracked ice

Place all ingredients into the Ninja pitcher. Put cover on the pitcher. Turn on Ninja and press speed 1 button. Blend for 15 seconds to 3 minutes or until contents are thoroughly blended. Press speed 1 button a second time to stop blending. Open pouring spout and add the ice. Close spout and blend again for 15 more seconds at speed 2. Pour contents into a cocktail glass and enjoy (yields about 1 1/2 cups).

6. Pineapple Parsley Vita Drink

1 cup pineapple juice

1 tablespoon lemon juice

1 cup tightly packed parsley

1 cup finely cracked ice

Put all ingredients into the Ninja pitcher. Put the cover on pitcher. Turn on Ninja and press speed 2 button. Run machine for 15 seconds to 1 minute. Serve immediately (yields about 1 1/2 pints).

7. Apple Juice Celery

1 cup apple juice

1 tablespoon lemon juice

1/2 cup celery leaves

1 cup finely cracked ice

Place all ingredients into the Ninja pitcher. Secure the lid. Power on the machine and press speed 2 button. Run Ninja for 15 seconds to 1 minute. Serve cold (yields about 1 1/2 pints).

8. Banana Strawberry Smoothie

2 ounces frozen strawberry sherbet

6 ounces fresh squeezed orange juice

4 ounces frozen strawberries

1 ripe banana

Combine all ingredients into the Ninja pitcher. Place the lid properly. Switch on the machine and long-press pulse buttons several times until you get your desired consistency. Serve on smoothie glass and top with a strawberry (yields two 8-ounce glasses).

9. Chilled But Hot Chocolate Smoothie

1 1/2 cup milk

1 1/2 tablespoons sugar

2 teaspoons packed chocolate mix

4 ounces semi sweet chocolate chips or milk chocolate chips

Chocolate shavings

Whipped cream

1 cup finely cracked ice

Melt chocolate chips over boiling water in a double boiler. Add sugar and hot chocolate mix, stirring continuously until mixture is smooth. Remove from heat and pour 1/2 cup of milk and it stir thoroughly. Let cool to room temperature. Pour chocolate mixture, ice, and the remaining milk into the Ninja pitcher. Secure the lid and turn on the machine. Long press pulse button several times until you have a semi frozen consistency. Pour contents into 2 large goblets, top whipped cream and sprinkle chocolate shavings.

10.   Frozen Mocha Smoothie

2 tablespoons chocolate syrup

3/4 cup fat-free milk

1/2 cup strong coffee

1 cup finely cracked ice

1/2 teaspoon artificial sweetener

Place all ingredients into the Ninja pitcher. Put the cover on the pitcher. Turn on Ninja and long-press pulse buttons several times until mixture is smooth. Serve on smoothie cups (yields two 10-ounce cups).

Scrumptious Soups and Sauces

11. Chicken Cordial Soup

2 cups chicken broth

2 eggs

1 tablespoon lemon juice

1/8 teaspoon salt

1 1/8 teaspoons pepper

2 tablespoons sherry

1 tablespoon chopped parsley

Heat chicken broth and set aside. Place eggs, lemon juice, salt, pepper, and sherry into the Ninja pitcher. Secure lid and turn on machine. Press speed 2 button and process mixture for 15 seconds. Open pouring spout and add hot chicken broth. Press pulse button 5 times. Pour into glass jar and chill. Serve cold garnished with chopped parsley (yields 1 1/2 pints).

12. Chicken Avocado Soup

2 1/2 cups chicken broth

2 cups sliced avocado

1 teaspoon salt

1 1/8 teaspoons pepper

2 tablespoons sherry

1/4 cup whipped cream

2 tablespoons sherry

1/4 cup whipping cream

2 tablespoons chopped pistachio nuts

Place all ingredients, except whipped cream and pistachio nuts, into the Ninja pitcher. Secure the lid. Turn on Ninja and press speed 1 button. Process the mixture for 30 seconds. Pour into glass jar and chill. Serve soup ice cold topped with whipped cream and pistachio nuts (yields 1 quart).

13. Carrot Vichyssoise

2 tablespoons butter

2 leeks, sliced

2 cups chicken broth

2 cups cooked diced carrots

1/2 teaspoon salt

1/8 teaspoon pepper

1/2 cup sweet cream

2 tablespoons chopped water cress leaves

Sauté leeks in butter over medium heat for 5 minutes. Add 1 cup of chicken broth and simmer for 15 minutes. Place sautéed leeks, the other cup of broth, carrots, and seasonings into the Ninja pitcher. Put cover on the pitcher. Turn on Ninja and press speed 1 button. Process mixture for 1 minute. Pour into glass jar and chill. Stir in cream, garnish with chopped water cress leaves, and serve cold or hot (yields 1 1/2 pints).

14. Pineapple Cucumber Soup

1 cup unsweetened pineapple juice

1 teaspoon gelatin

2 tablespoons cold water

2 cups coarsely diced, raw, unpeeled cucumber

4 sprays raw parsley

1/4 teaspoon salt

Soak gelatin in cold water, melt in a double boiler, and set aside. Place all ingredients into the Ninja pitcher in the order indicated. Put cover on the pitcher. Turn on machine and blend at speed 1 for 15 seconds to 2 minutes. Pour contents into refrigerator tray and chill for 1 hour. Before serving, transfer soup into Ninja pitcher and blend again in pulse for smooth texture (yields about 1 pint).

15. Black Bean Savory Soup

2 tablespoons fat

1/4 cup diced onion

1/4 cup diced celery

1/4 cup diced green pepper

1 cup cooked kidney beans

1 cup kidney bean liquor

1 cup tomato juice

2 teaspoon salt

1 hard boiled egg, sliced

1 lemon, sliced

Sauté first four ingredients in fat until onions are golden brown. Place sauté, kidney beans, and bean liquor into the Ninja pitcher. Place the lid properly and press Power button. Process mixture at speed 2 for 20 seconds. Heat tomato juice in a large sauce pot placed over medium heat. Add blended mixture and heat thoroughly. Garnish with slices of egg and lemon, and serve (yields 1 1/2 pints).

16. Shrimp Bisque

1 pint milk

1 tablespoon flour

15

2 tablespoons butter

1 teaspoon salt

1 1/8 teaspoons pepper

2/3 cup cooked or canned shrimp

Few sprays raw parsley

Place all ingredients into the Ninja pitcher in the order indicated. Secure the lid and turn on the machine. Run Ninja at speed 1 for 15 seconds. Heat mixture in double boiler, sauce pot, or skillet, stirring occasionally. Serve hot (yields 2 1/2 cups).

17. Hollandaise Sauce

3 egg yolks

2 tablespoons lemon juice

1 spray parsley

1/2 teaspoon salt

Dash pepper

1/2 cup butter

1/2 cup boiling hot water

Place all ingredients except boiling water into the Ninja pitcher (butter should be at room temperature). Secure the lid. Turn on Ninja and press speed 1 button. Open pouring spout and gradually pour water into the pitcher. Close spout and time machine for 1 minute. Cook mixture over hot water, stirring constantly, to the consistency of soft custard. Serve hot (yields 1 pint).

18.Creole Sauce

3 tablespoons fat

1 green pepper, diced

1 can condensed tomato soup

2 whole canned pimentos

1/2 clove garlic

1 teaspoon salt

Dash pepper

2 tablespoons sherry

Sauté green pepper in fat over medium heat until fork-tender. Place sauté and the remaining ingredients into the Ninja pitcher. Place the lid properly. Press Power button and then speed 1 button. Process mixture for about 1 minute. Pour contents into sauce pot and cook over direct heat. Serve hot with cooked shrimp, meat or fish (yields 1 pint).

19. Bechamel Sauce

2 tablespoons fat

2 tablespoons chopped onion

1/2 cup chicken broth

1 spray celery leaves

1 tablespoon flour

1/2 cup cream

Sauté chopped onion in fat over medium heat until onions are golden brown. Place sauté and all other ingredients, except cream, into the Ninja pitcher. Secure the lid. Switch on the Ninja and blend at speed 1 for 1 minute. Stir in cream and serve over hot vegetables (yields 1 cup).

20. Italian-style Beef Entrée Sauce

4 tablespoons fat

1/2 lb ground raw beef

1/2 cup celery leaves

1/2 cup sliced green peppers

1/2 cup sliced onion

1/2 small garlic clove

2 1/2 cups canned tomatoes

1 teaspoon salt

3 tablespoons canned tomato paste

Sauté ground beef in fat, stirring constantly, over medium heat for about 5 minutes and set aside. Sauté celery leaves, green pepper, onion, and garlic in fat until tender. Place sauté vegetables, tomatoes, tomato paste, and salt into the Ninja pitcher. Put the lid on the pitcher and turn on machine. Blend for 20 seconds. Pour blended mixture in a sauce pot. Add sautéed beef and simmer, without the cover, over low heat for 25 minutes or until sauce thickens, stirring occasionally. Serve hot with cooked rice or spaghetti and sprinkled with grated parmesan cheese (yields 1 pint).

Baking Delights

21.Cranberry Muffins

2 cups flour

2 teaspoons baking powder

1/2 teaspoon soda

1/2 teaspoon salt

7/8 cup milk

1 egg

1/3 cup shortening

1/2 cup sugar

1 cup raw cranberries

Sift flour, baking powder, soda, and salt in separate mixing bowl. Place the remaining ingredients into the Ninja pitcher in the order indicated. Secure the lid on the pitcher. Turn on machine and press speed 1 button. Blend for 15 to 30 seconds. Stir blended mixture into the sifting bowl in flour mixture. Place batter in greased muffin pans and bake in oven set to 400 degrees Fahrenheit for about 25 minutes. Serve (yields 18 muffins).

22.   Pain Popovers

7/8 cup milk

2 eggs

1 tablespoon fat

1/4 teaspoon salt

Combine all ingredients into the Ninja pitcher in the order indicated. Put cover on the pitcher and switch on Ninja. Press speed 1 button and time machine for 20 seconds. Transfer blended mixture to muffin pans and bake at 425 degrees Fahrenheit for about 45 minutes. Serve warm (yields 8 popovers).

23.   Coconut Waffles

2 cups flour

4 teaspoons baking powder

1/2 teaspoon salt

1 1/2 cups shredded coconut

1 3/4 cups milk

2 eggs

6 tablespoon fat

Sift flour, salt and baking powder into separate mixing bowl and set aside. Place remaining ingredients into the Ninja pitcher and secure the lid. Turn on machine and press speed 2 button. Run Ninja for 15 seconds or until contents are thoroughly blended. Pour blended mixture slowly into sifted for and stir to smoothness. Griddle dough and serve (yields 24 4-inch waffles).

24. Almond Tea Cakes

1 1/2 cups flour

1/4 teaspoon salt

3 teaspoons baking powder

1/2 cup milk

2 egg whites

1/2 cup salted, toasted almonds

1/2 teaspoon vanilla

1/2 teaspoon almond extract

1/3 cup shortening

3/4 cup sugar

Sift flour, salt, and baking powder in a mixing bowl and set aside. Place remaining ingredients into the Ninja pitcher and place the lid properly. Press speed 2 and run Ninja for 15 seconds. Pour mixture slowly into sifted flour and stir until smooth. Place dough onto muffin pans and bake at 375 degrees Fahrenheit for 20 minutes. Serve (yields 30 cupcakes).

25.   Raisin Pudding

2 cups flour

1 teaspoon baking powder

1/2 teaspoon soda

1/4 teaspoon salt

1 cup water

1 egg

1/3 cup shortening

1 cup brown sugar

2 cups soaked raisins

1 teaspoon cinnamon or 1/4 teaspoon nutmeg or dash Angostura

Sift flour, baking powder, soda, and salt into a mixing bowl. Put remaining ingredients into the Ninja pitcher and place the lid properly. Turn on machine, press speed 1 button, and process for 15 to 30 seconds. Pour blended mixture into sifted flour and beat to smoothness. Place dough onto large greased muffin pans. Bake at 350 degrees Fahrenheit for 30 minutes. Serve with any pudding sauce.

26.   Fruit Molasses Cookies

3 cups flour

2 teaspoons baking powder

1/2 teaspoon soda

1/2 teaspoon salt

1 teaspoon cinnamon

1/2 teaspoon nutmeg

1/2 teaspoon cloves

1/4 cup sour milk or buttermilk

1/2 cup molasses

1 egg

1 unpressed cup seedless raisins

1/2 cup shortening

1/4 cup brown sugar

Sift first 7 ingredients in a mixing bowl and set aside. Place the remaining ingredients into the Ninja pitcher. Cover pitcher and turn on machine. Press pulse button several times until raisins are broken. Pour mixture into sifted ingredients and beat to smoothness. Chill dough. Knead dough on a slightly floured board into 1/8-inch thick. Cut dough into desired shapes and place cookies on baking sheet. Bake at 375 degrees Fahrenheit for 12 minutes (yields 100 small cookies).

27.   Oatmeal Hermit Cookies

1 1/2 cups flour

2 teaspoons baking powder

1/2 teaspoon salt

1/2 teaspoon cinnamon

1/2 cup chopped nut meats

1/2 cup milk

2 eggs

1/2 cup shortening

2 cups raw oatmeal

1/2 teaspoon vanilla extract

1 cup sugar

1 cup raisins

Sift flour, baking powder, and salt into a mixing bowl and set aside. Place remaining ingredients into the Ninja pitcher. Secure the lid. Turn on machine and run for 15 seconds at speed 1. Pour blended mixture into sifted ingredients and whip until you have a smooth batter. Heap spoonfuls of the batter onto a baking sheet and bake at 375 degrees Fahrenheit for 10 minutes (yields 4 dozens 2-inch cookies).

28.   Cocoroons

1 1/2 cups flour

1/4 teaspoon salt

3 teaspoon baking powder

1 egg

3/4 cup sugar

1/4 cup milk

1 cup shredded coconut

1/3 cup butter

1/8 teaspoon almond extract

Sift flour, salt, and baking powder into a mixing bowl. Put remaining ingredients into the Ninja pitcher and press Power button. Secure lid and press speed 1 button. Run Ninja for 15 seconds. Gradually pour blended mixture into sifted flour and beat until smooth. Heap teaspoonfuls of the dough into a baking sheet and bake at 350 degrees Fahrenheit for 15 minutes (yields 4 dozen cookies).

29.　　Grape Raisin Pie

2 cups seedless raisins

1/2 cup water

1 tablespoon gelatin

1/4 cup honey

1/4 cup grape juice

1 tablespoon lemon juice

1 cup heavy cream

Simmer raisins in water in covered pan for 5 minutes. Soak gelatin in cold water and add to raisins. Place raisin-gelatin and the remaining ingredients, except cream, into the Ninja pitcher. Put the cover on the pitcher. Turn on machine and press pulse button five times. Chill mixture in refrigerator until mixture stiffens. Remove from refrigerator and fill in with whipped cream. Transfer into baked pie shell and chill for 3 hours. Garnish with whipped cream, if desired, and serve.

30.　　Cheese Torte

1/2 cup light cream

2 eggs

2 cups cottage cheese

2 tablespoons lemon juice

1 teaspoon vanilla extract

2/3 cup sugar

1/4 teaspoon salt

3 tablespoons flour

1 cup Graham cracker crumbs

4 tablespoons butter

2 tablespoons sugar

Place first 5 ingredients into the Ninja pitcher in the order indicated. Secure the lid properly and press Power button. Long-press pulse button several times until contents are thoroughly blended. In a separate mixing bowl, whisk butter, Graham cracker crumbs, and sugar. Pat butter mixture in the bottom of a 9-inch layer cake pan. Add blended mixture and bake at 325 degrees Fahrenheit for about 1 hour.

Appetizing Spreads, Salads and Salad Dressings

31.Carrot Spread

1/3 cup mayonnaise

1 1/2 cups diced carrots

1 teaspoon salt

1/2 bunch chopped water cress

Place all ingredients except water cress into the Ninja pitcher. Put cover on the pitcher and turn on machine. Press speed 2 button and process for 2 minutes or until contents are thoroughly blended. Pour blended mixture into bowl. Stir in water cress and chill to attain spreading consistency. Spread in toast fingers or canapé biscuits or use as sandwich filling (yields 1 cup).

32.   Shrimp Paste

1/4 cup chili sauce

1/4 cup mayonnaise

2 tablespoons melon juice

1/2 teaspoon salt

1/8 teaspoon dry mustard

1 lb cooked whole shrimp

1/2 bunch chopped water cress

Put all ingredients except water cress into the Ninja pitcher and secure the lid. Turn on Ninja and press speed 2 button. Process contents for 2 minutes then pour into a bowl. Add the water cress and stir thoroughly. Chill to attain spreading consistency. Spread onto bread or biscuits.

33. Mock Pâté de Foie Gras

1/3 cup evaporated milk

1/3 cup salad oil

1 tablespoon lemon juice

1 teaspoon Worcestershire sauce

1/2 lb diced, cooked chicken, beef, calves or pork liver

4 sprays raw parsley

1 teaspoon salt

Make sure all ingredients are at room temperature. Place them all into the Ninja pitcher in the order indicated. Place the lid correctly and switch on Ninja. Press speed 2 button and time machine for 2 minutes or until contents are blended well. Pour contents into jar and chill to attain spreading consistency. Spread onto toasted bread or biscuits (yields 1 1/2 cups).

34.   Cucumber Salad

1 tablespoon gelatin

4 tablespoon cold water

1/3 cup room temperature water

2 tablespoon lemon juice

2 cups sliced, unpeeled raw cucumber

1/2 small onion

4 sprays raw parsley

1 teaspoon salt

Soak gelatin in cold water and melt over boiling water. Place other ingredients into the Ninja pitcher in the order indicated. Add gelatin and place the lid correctly. Turn on Ninja and press pulse button five times. Chill mixture until it begins to stiffen. Transfer into 3 cup ring mold or into 6 individual molds and chill again. Serve on a plate with lettuce leaves garnished with mayonnaise or sour cream.

35. Shrimp Salad

12 ounces cooked or canned shrimps

1 tablespoon gelatin

1/4 cup cold water

1 1/2 cups evaporated milk

2 tablespoons lemon juice

1 1/2 teaspoons salt

1 teaspoon paprika

1 teaspoon dry mustard

1 slice thin onion

2 sprays raw parsley

2 sprays raw celery leaves

1/2 cup heavy (or light) cream

Remove and discard intestinal vein from shrimps. Soak gelatin in cold water and melt over boiling water. Pour milk and other ingredients except cream into the Ninja pitcher. Add shrimp and gelatin. Place lid properly and press Power button. Press speed 2 button and run for about 2 minutes. Pour blended mixture into a bowl and stir in whipped cream. Transfer in well-oiled quart mold or 6 individual molds. Chill until firm. Serve on lettuce leaves garnished with mayonnaise.

36.   Cabbage Salad

1 tablespoon gelatin

1/4 cup cold water

1 cup water

2 tablespoons lemon juice

1/2 teaspoon salt

1 teaspoon sugar

1 cup coarsely diced cabbage

1 cup diced celery

4 sprays raw parsley

Soak gelatin in cold water and melt over hot water. Place other ingredients into the Ninja pitcher in the order indicated. Add gelatin and place the lid properly. Turn on machine and press pulse button five times so that contents are partially blended. Chill until mixture begins to stiffen. Pour into 3 cup mold and chill again until firm. Serve on lettuce leaves garnished with mayonnaise.

37. Mineral Oil Mayonnaise Dressing

1 whole egg

2 tablespoon lemon juice or vinegar

1/2 teaspoon dry mustard

1/2 teaspoon salt

1 cup mineral oil

Combine egg, vinegar or lemon juice, seasonings, and 1/4 cup of the oil in the Ninja pitcher in the order indicated. Secure the lid. Press Power button and process mixture at speed 1 for 5 seconds or until contents are well-blended. Open pouring sprout and add oil gradually and long-press pulse button. Spoon dressing into salad (yields about 1 1/4 cups).

38. Ninja Clover Leaf Dressing

1 1/2 cups salad oil

1/2 cup vinegar

1 small can tomato soup

2 tablespoons sugar

1 teaspoon dry mustard

1 teaspoon salt

1 teaspoon paprika

1 tablespoon Worcestershire sauce

1 tablespoon diced onion

1 teaspoon dry mustard

1/4 clove garlic

1/4 raw green pepper

Place all ingredients into the Ninja pitcher in the order indicated. Put cover on the pitcher. Turn on Ninja and press speed 1 button. Run Ninja for about 1 minute. Spoon onto salad. Note: Vinegar or wine may be used instead of lemon juice.

39.   Roquefort Salad Dressing

1 cup salad oil

3 tablespoons lemon juice

1 teaspoon sugar

1 teaspoon sugar

2 teaspoons paprika

1 tablespoon diced white onion

3 ounces Roquefort cheese

Put all ingredients into the Ninja pitcher in the order indicated and secure the lid. Turn on machine and process mixture at speed 2 for about 1 minute. Stir in vegetable salad.

40.   Herbal French-style Dressing

3/4 cup salad oil

1/4 cup lemon juice

1/2 cup drained canned apricots or pineapple

1/4 cup canned fruit juice or 1/4 cup port wine

1/2 teaspoon salt

Combine all ingredients into the Ninja pitcher in the order indicated. Place lid correctly and press Power button. Press pulse button five times. Pour dressing on lettuce salad (yields 1 to 1 1/2 cups).

Extraordinary Desserts

41.Apricot Custard

1 pint milk

2/3 cup soaked, dried apricots

1/2 cup sugar

2 eggs

Place all ingredients into the Ninja pitcher in the order indicated. Place lid correctly. Press the Power button and then the speed 2 button. Run Ninja for 10 seconds or until contents are blended well. Pour contents onto greased mustard cups. Place cups in a pan of hot water and bake at 350 degrees Fahrenheit for about 25 minutes. Top with whipped cream and serve either hot or cold (serves 4).

42.   Apple Sauce

1 cup water

2 cups diced, cored unpeeled apples

1/2 cup sugar

Pour water into the Ninja pitcher. Add apples and sugar. Place the lid properly. Turn on Ninja and long-press pulse button several times until contents are thoroughly blended. Pour blended mixture into a saucepan and bring to boil. Serve hot or cold (serves 4).

43.   Orange Bread Pudding

1 cup orange juice

Thin yellow peel of 1/2 orange

2 eggs

1/3 cup sugar

1/4 cup butter

1/4 teaspoon salt

1 3/4 cups hot evaporated milk

2 cups soft bread cubes

1 cup raisins

Place orange juice and orange peel into the Ninja pitcher. Secure the lid. Turn on machine and press pulse button five times or until contents are thoroughly blended. Remove lid and add eggs, sugar, butter, and salt. Replace cover and press speed 3 button. Run machine for 1 minute. In a greased 1 quart casserole, mix blended mixture, hot milk, bread cubes, and raisins. Place in pan of water and bake at 325 degrees Fahrenheit for one hour. Serve (yields 1 quart).

44.   Caramel Rice Pudding

1 cup milk

1 egg

1 cup raisins

2 tablespoons brown sugar

1/8 teaspoon salt

1 cup cooked rice

Combine all ingredients except rice into the Ninja pitcher in the order indicated. Put cover on the pitcher. Turn on Ninja and press pulse button until contents are thoroughly blended. Pour mixture in a bowl. Add rice and mix. Transfer contents into four greased custard cups. Place in a pan of hot water and bake at 350 degrees Fahrenheit for 30 minutes.

45.   Apricot Bavarian Cream

1 tablespoon gelatin

1/4 cup cold water

1 1/2 cups unsweetened pineapple juice

2/3 cup soaked dried apricot

4 tablespoons sugar

1 cup heavy cream

Soak gelatin in cold water and melt over boiling water. Put all ingredients except cream into the Ninja pitcher in the order indicated. Place lid. Turn on machine and press speed 1 button. Run Ninja for 1 minute or until contents are well-blended. Pour into bowl and chill until mixture begins to stiffen. Fill mixture with whipped cream, pour into molds, and chill until firm. Garnish with whipped cream and chopped almonds and serve (serves 6).

46.   Strawberry Gelatin

1 pack strawberry gelatin

1 cup hot water

2 tablespoons lemon juice

1 pint fresh strawberries

1/3 cup sugar or 8 ounces frozen strawberries

Dissolve gelatin in hot liquid. Cool gelatin to lukewarm. Pour gelatin into the Ninja pitcher. Add remaining ingredients in the order indicated. Secure the lid. Press Power button and then speed 3 button button. Run machine until contents are thoroughly blended. Pour mixture into loaf pan and chill until firm. Cut into squares and serve in sherbet glasses (yields 1 pint).

47.   Pineapple Sherbet

1/2 tablespoon gelatin

4 tablespoons cold water

1 cup milk or light cream

1 cup diced canned pineapple

2 tablespoons lemon juice

3 tablespoons sugar

Soak gelatin in cold water and melt over hot water. Pour gelatin and remaining ingredients into the Ninja pitcher. Put lid on the pitcher. Turn on the machine and press the speed 3 button for 20 seconds. Pour mixture into refrigerator tray, stirring occasionally, and freeze (serves 4).

48.   Apple Ginger Sherbet

1/2 tablespoons gelatin

4 tablespoons cold water

2 1/2 cups applesauce

1 tablespoon preserved ginger or 1/8 teaspoon dried ginger

2 tablespoons lemon juice

Soak gelatin in cold water and melt over hot water. Place all ingredients into the Ninja pitcher in the order indicated. Secure the lid. Press Power button and then speed 3 button. Process mixture for 1 minute. Transfer contents to refrigerator tray and freeze. Serve on sherbet glasses (serves 6).

49. Butter Pecan Ice Cream

1 cup evaporated milk

1 pack vanilla ice cream mix

3 tablespoons dark brown sugar

1/2 cup roasted, salted pecans

1 teaspoon vanilla extract

2 cups whipped cream

Combine all ingredients except whipped cream into the Ninja pitcher. Place the lid correctly. Turn on Ninja and press speed 1 button. Process mixture for 1 minute. Pour mixture into refrigerator tray and freeze until mushy. Add whipped cream to partially frozen mixture and stir to smoothness. Freeze before serving.

50. Coffee Ice Cream

1 cup cold coffee

24 marshmallows

1 teaspoon vanilla extract

Dash salt

Dash Angostura

1 cup whipped cream

Place all ingredients into the Ninja pitcher. Secure the lid and turn on machine. Press speed 1 button, blending mixture for about 1 minute. Partially freeze blended mixture in the freezer. Then, stir in whipped cream. Freeze thoroughly before serving.

Conclusion

Thank you again for downloading this book!

I hope this book was able to provide you with easy-to-do delectable recipes for your high-performance Ninja Professional Blender.

The next step is to try anything you've got at home right now to experiment with Ninja.

Finally, if you enjoyed this book, please take the time to share your thoughts and post a review on Amazon. It'd be greatly appreciated!

Thank you and good luck!

Made in the USA
Middletown, DE
29 September 2015